MYTHOLOGY and LEGENDS around the WORLD

The Myths and Legends of the Middle East

Edited by Joanne Randolph

Cavendish Square
New York

Published in 2018 by Cavendish Square Publishing, LLC
243 5th Avenue, Suite 136, New York, NY 10016

First Edition

Website: cavendishsq.com

Library of Congress Cataloging-in-Publication Data

Names: Randolph, Joanne, editor.
Title: The myths and legends of the Middle East / edited by Joanne Randolph.
Description: New York : Cavendish Square Publishing, 2018. | Series: Mythology and legends around the world | Includes glossary and index. | Audience: Grades 3-6.
Identifiers: ISBN 9781502632791 (library bound) | ISBN 9781502634498 (pbk.) | ISBN 9781502633064 (ebook)
Subjects: LCSH: Mythology, Middle Eastern--Juvenile literature.
Classification: LCC BL1060.R36 2018 | DDC 398.20939'4--dc23

Editorial Director: David McNamara
Editor: Caitlyn Miller
Copy Editor: Rebecca Rohan
Associate Art Director: Amy Greenan
Designer: Megan Metté
Production Coordinator: Karol Szymczuk
Photo Research: J8 Media

"Tales from Mesopotamia" by Rosalie F. Baker from *Calliope* Magazine (October 2006)
"Enki and the Flood" retold by Heather M. Hopkins from *Appleseeds* Magazine (October 2004)
"Wise Fools" by Robert D. San Souci from *Appleseeds* Magazine (November 2003)
"The Arabian Nights: The Tale of the Fisherman and the Genie" retold by F.M. Black from *Calliope* Magazine (February 2000)
"The Traveler's Treasures" by Elisabeth Greenberg from *Faces* Magazine (November 2001)
"The King Who Wanted to Fly: A Persian Legend from the Shah Nameh" retold by Marilyn Bolchunos from *Cricket* Magazine (January 2007)
"Hodja and the Hungry Coat: A Turkish Tale" retold by Gale Sypher Jacob from *Spider* Magazine (February 2007)

The photographs in this book are used by permission and through the courtesy of: Cover AF Fotographie/Alamy Stock Photo; p. 4 Nexus 7/Shutterstock.com; p. 6 Pingebat/Shutterstock.com; p. 7 Ivy Close Images/Alamy Stock Photo; p. 9 Bettmann/Getty Images; p. 10 Print Collector/Hulton Archive/Getty Images; p. 12-13 Ileana_bt/Shutterstock.com; p. 14, 44 Historical Picture Archive/Corbis/Getty Images; p. 17 Cyrustr/Shutterstock.com; p. 20 Matthew Clemente/Shutterstock.com; p. 22 Bamboovn/Shutterstock.com; p. 23 Yevlem/Wikimedia Commons/File:(ar-Rashid) dirham 170h.jpg/CC BY SA 3.0; p. 24 Scheherazade et le Calife/CCI/Bridgeman Images; p. 26-27 Stocksnapper/Shutterstock.com; p. 29 Kazakova Maryia/Shutterstock.com; p. 32 Heritage Images/Hulton Archive/Getty Images; p. 36-37 Antoine2K/Shutterstock.com; p. 38 Okeyphotos/iStock/Thinkstock.com; p. 43 Javarman/Shutterstock.com; p. 49 IgorGolovniov/Shutterstock.com; p. 50 Wikimedia Commons/File:KavoosAir.jpg/Public Domain; p. 54-55 Real Monasterio de El Escorial, El Escorial, Spain/Bridgeman Images; p. 59 Elena Veselova/Shutterstock.com.

Printed in the United States of America

Contents

1 Middle Eastern Myths and Legends

The Middle East is a dry, hot region on our planet, east of the African continent. It includes such countries as Iran, Iraq, Turkey, and Saudi Arabia. People have lived in the Middle East for thousands of years. In fact, the area between the Tigris and Euphrates Rivers, in present-day Iran (once called Persia), is called the "cradle of civilization" because it was the first place where more-complex communities developed. As with any ancient culture, early Middle Eastern peoples developed myths and legends to help them explain the creation of Earth, their culture, and different natural phenomena.

Tales from Mesopotamia

The Babylonian Story of Creation

The following is a **Babylonian** story about how Earth came to be. In the beginning, there was Chaos, a huge,

Opposite: The sunken village of Halfeti, in Turkey, has existed for thousands of years. It was partially submerged when a dam was built in the late 1990s.

This map shows, in shades of dark green, the countries that are generally considered to be part of the Middle East.

boundless, watery mass. Apsu was the fresh water, and Tiamat was the salt water. Their children—Anu, Enlil, and Ea—brought order to the world. Anu took charge of the heavens, Enlil ruled the air and later the earth, and Ea controlled the waters and the abyss that they believed surrounded the earth. Apsu and Tiamat plotted to destroy their offspring. In the fierce struggle that ensued, Ea killed Apsu and laid the ancient deity to rest beneath the earth.

The earth rejoiced in its new order, and Ea returned to his temple at Eridu. There his son, the learned Marduk, was born. Yet, all was not well, for Tiamat raged within

Marduk (*right*) is shown with his thunderbolt raised as he fights Tiamat, the symbol for chaos.

herself at the loss of Apsu. To avenge his death, she created an army of eleven horrible monsters, with the invincible Kingu as leader.

Ea summoned the gods to a banquet. As the music flowed, the question of how to defeat Tiamat arose. Young Marduk offered to meet Tiamat in hand-to-hand combat, but he had one condition. If he was successful, he was to have supreme authority over all the gods. Despite their eagerness to see Tiamat defeated, the gods decided to test Marduk's powers and commanded him to make a particular **constellation** of stars disappear and then reappear. When Marduk succeeded, the gods eagerly accepted this condition.

Armed with a net, the four winds, a thunderbolt, a storm, and weapons the gods had given him, Marduk snared Tiamat before she could use any of her magic powers. Tiamat opened her mouth to engulf the upstart god in flames, but Marduk filled her gaping jaws with one of the winds. As the wind rushed through Tiamat's form, swelling and distending it, Marduk pierced her swollen body with a spear and killed her. Chaos was dead, and order and organization reigned.

The world was ready to be created. Marduk stood above Tiamat's body and cut it in half. With one part, he

Marduk is shown here with his sacred animal, the dragon.

made the vault of heaven; with the other, he created the earth.

The world again rejoiced in its new order. Then, the gods realized they needed people to sacrifice to them. After much discussion, Marduk summoned the imprisoned Kingu. From his blood, Marduk fashioned the human race. To express their gratitude for the gift of humans, the gods built a shrine and temple honoring Marduk at Babylon, Marduk's favorite site.

Note: This version of the creation tale is from the ruler Hammurabi's time (circa 1750 BCE), when Marduk was worshiped as the chief god. It was found on the Seven Tablets of Creation, large portions of which are preserved in London's British Museum. As several tablets are broken, historians must make educated guesses about the missing text.

Opposite: This stone tablet is part of the Code of Hammurabi.

Inanna is shown standing on the backs of two lionesses. Her power led her to be associated with lions.

Inanna, a Sumerian Goddess

The most important goddess in the **pantheon** of **Sumer** was Inanna, the goddess of love and fertility. Her name means "lady of the sky." According to Sumerian mythology, Inanna's most famous exploit involved her determination to unseat her sister Ereshkigal, the goddess of the underworld and death. When Inanna was told that she could enter the realm of the dead only if she removed one item of clothing at each of the seven entrances, she agreed, and arrived to face her sister naked. Undaunted, Inanna pulled Ereshkigal from her throne and sat down. For these willful acts, the judges of death condemned her to die by hanging.

After many pleas by Inanna's handmaiden, the judges relented and granted Inanna a safe return to earth, but only if she found a substitute to accept the punishment for her "crime." Inanna agreed, but she refused every friend's offer to take her place. When she reached the palace at Uruk and saw her husband rejoicing instead of mourning her death, Inanna immediately named him as her substitute.

2 Enki and the Flood

The tradition of a great flood is common to the literature of many civilizations. While the Mesopotamian story is usually credited as the earliest, it is uncertain whether there was a relationship among the various tales; however, geologists have proven that the Tigris and Euphrates rivers did periodically overflow their banks. Perhaps one flood was so catastrophic that it formed the basis for the Babylonian tale known as "The Great Flood."

Hard-working Gods

Many years ago, before the mother goddess created humans, the gods did all the work on earth. They pressed their spades into the soil, dug the Tigris and Euphrates Rivers, and shaped the lifelines of the land. For 3,600

Opposite: This depiction of the great Babylonian flood was created by Ernest Wallcousins for a 1915 collection of myths from Babylonia and Assyria.

years, they groaned and grumbled. Until, one day, they could stand the work no more. When they told their leader, Enlil, of their trouble, he shed a heavy tear.

"Mami," Enlil called to the mother goddess, "create a mortal man. He will bear the gods' workload. He will make the heavens peaceful once again."

So Mami took the blood and wisdom of the heavens and mixed it with Earth's clay. She chanted and spit upon it. A drumbeat filled the land. When humankind appeared, the gods knelt at Mami's feet and cried, "At last, the heavens will be peaceful once again!"

What a Racket!

Six hundred years passed, and the gods were unhappy once again. Humankind was too noisy. Their work was louder than a bellowing bull.

"I cannot sleep with this racket," Enlil said. "The noise of humankind has become too much. Send sickness to the people," he told the gods. "Make the country peaceful once again."

Disease spread throughout the earth. Fever blew in like a storm. Finally, a wise man, Atrahasis (called Utnapishtim in one version of the story), called to Enki, "God of water, ease our pain!"

The story of Enki and the great flood was likely created as a way for the people of Babylon to make sense of the extreme weather in the region.

And so Enki, the god of water, brought relief to humankind.

The Trouble Continues

Another six hundred years passed, and the gods grew restless of the racket once again. Enlil called out to Adad, the god of storms, "Adad, wipe away your rain!"

And so a great drought fell upon the earth. Clouds gathered but did not shed a drop of rain. Atrahasis could stand it no longer and called again to Enki, "God of water, ease our pain!"

And so Enki brought relief to humankind once more. But another six hundred years passed, and the gods grew restless of the racket once again. To the goddess of the harvest, Enlil said, "Nissaba, stop producing grain."

And so starvation swept the earth. Seeds failed to sprout. Finally, Atrahasis called to Enki once more, "God of water, ease our pain!"

This time, Enki shrugged his shoulders. "I cannot wipe away your pain. Enlil will not stand the racket. He has ordered me to send great rains, floodwaters to wipe away humans so the earth is peaceful once again.

"But listen closely to my message," Enki said. "Build a boat to survive the rain. After seven days and seven nights, the flood will finish flowing and you will live peacefully once again."

Atrahasis Succeeds

Atrahasis gathered his family together. They built a sturdy boat. On board they loaded birds, fish, and animals. Then they waited for the rain. Soon, the darkness became total. Adad bellowed from the sky. Wind screamed throughout the earth. The floodwaters stampeded over the land like a bull.

Seven days and seven nights passed. Finally, Atrahasis no longer heard the rain. When he poked his head out the door, sunlight spread over his face once again. Rejoicing, Atrahasis released his family and animals to roam about the drying land.

But Atrahasis, the wise man, would always remember the past. "Sing of the flood to all people," he told his children, "when humans survived the rain." And from that day to the present, his children did the same.

3 Wise Fools

A popular figure in Muslim storytelling is the wise fool. The fool appears as different people in different stories. In these two stories, we see him first as Goha, then as Abu Nuwas, the poet.

Goha and His Son

Goha's son was afraid to do or say anything, for fear people would disagree with him. "We will go to the next village," said Goha, "and I will show you that the only foolishness is worrying what others think."

Goha saddled his donkey and set out, with his son walking behind. People pointed and said, "What a heartless man to ride while his boy walks."

So Goha traded places with his son. Now people sneered, "What a disrespectful son to ride while his poor father walks."

Opposite: Donkeys have been popular beasts of burden throughout history and feature in many stories.

In the story of Abu Nuwas and the Hundred Eggs, a ruler gives 100 members of his court an egg to hide.

Then Goha climbed up behind his son. "How cruel to make that little donkey carry two riders!" exclaimed passers-by.

At this, Goha and his son climbed down, walking behind the donkey. "What fools!" onlookers cried. "They walk when they could ride!"

At last, they decided to carry the donkey. As the people laughed at them, Goha said, "You see, my son, whatever you do, you will never please everyone, so what is the use of worrying about it?"

Abu Nuwas and the Hundred Eggs

Abu Nuwas, the poet, was companion and court jester to the famous ruler **Caliph** Harun Al Rasheed. As jester, his job was to amuse the caliph. They often played tricks on each other.

One day, the caliph gave an egg to each of 100 members of his court, ordering each to hide the egg in his lap. When Abu Nuwas entered and took his seat, the caliph said, "I order each of you to show your loyalty by laying an egg for me this morning."

Each of the hundred courtiers held up his egg, except for Abu Nuwas. Hiding a smile, the caliph asked the poet, "Do you refuse to obey?"

To his surprise, Abu Nuwas threw back his head and crowed so loudly that everyone covered their ears to silence the sound.

"What is the matter with you?" asked the caliph.

"O Master! With a hundred hens, surely you need at least one rooster!"

At this, the ruler began to laugh. Then he rewarded his friend with 100 gold coins for his amusing answer.

This old coin, a silver dirham, was minted in Madinat al-Salam, which is today called Baghdad.

4 The *Arabian Nights*: The Tale of the Fisherman and the Genie

Long ago in Persia, there lived two kings who were brothers. Each of their wives was unfaithful to them. The eldest brother decided to marry a different woman each night and to slay her in the morning, so she would have no chance to be unfaithful. Every day, the king's vizier (a high-ranking government official) supplied him with another woman to entertain him. One time, the eldest daughter of the vizier told her father to send her to spend the night with the king. The vizier argued vehemently against such a plan, but she insisted that he do so. Reluctantly, the vizier gave his daughter, Scheherazade, to the king and said, "May Allah not

Opposite: Scheherazade tells the caliph a story in this illustration from a 1920s edition of *1001 Arabian Nights* that was published in France.

KIRGHEZ
CASPIAN SEA
SEA OF ARAL
BOKHARA
Khiva
KHIVA
R. AMOO DARIA OR OXUS
DESERT
Bokhara
Samarkand
R. Attruck
Balkh
Teheran
PERSIA
Herat
Ispahan
AFGHANIS
BELOOCHISTAN
PERSIAN GUL
40
30

This 1875 map shows the Middle East, including Persia, which has been called Iran since 1935.

deprive me of you." But Scheherazade had a plan, a plan that involved telling the king a different story each night, thereby delaying her death and preventing others from being killed.

Scheherazade's Tales Begin

One night, Scheherazade said to the king:

> I heard, O king, that there once lived an old, poor fisherman, who could hardly provide food for his wife and three daughters. One day he cast his net four times into the sea. The first time he hauled in a dead donkey. Another toss netted a jug filled with sand and mud. A third cast was hard to pull up ("I must have caught a very big fish," he thought), but it only contained a jumble of broken pots and garbage. He wept and wondered how he would ever be able to support his loved ones. He prayed to Allah to be good to him and flung out his net one last time. When he tried to haul it in, it was so heavy that he could hardly move it. He then swam out and dove down to unfasten his tangled net. When he was able to gather it in, he found a large, long-necked, brass jar with a lead stopper bearing the seal of King Solomon. "I'll sell it in the market," he thought to himself, rejoicing. "It will be worth at least two measures of wheat."
>
> But, when he tried to remove it, the jar wouldn't budge, so he decided to pry off the stopper and

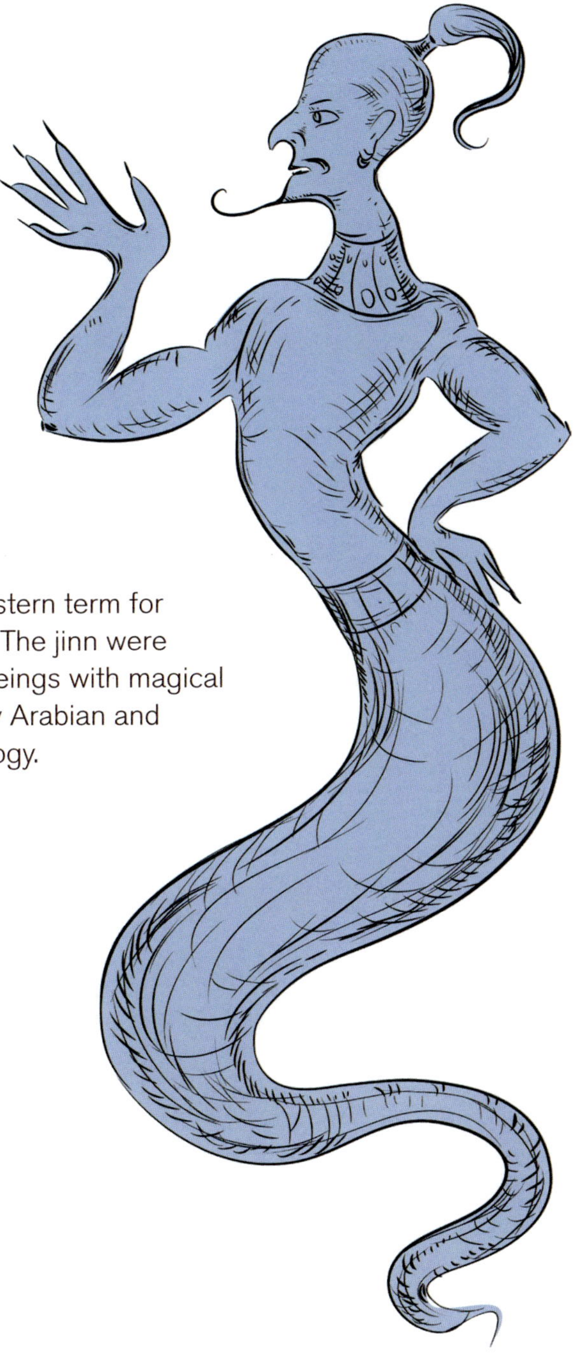

The Middle Eastern term for genie is "jinni." The jinn were supernatural beings with magical powers in early Arabian and Islamic mythology.

empty it out. A little plume of smoke soon began to emerge from the opening of the brass jar. It spread out wide in the sky and slowly formed itself into a terrible-looking, giant genie. The fisherman was speechless; he was terribly afraid.

"I bring you good news," said the genie. "I will kill you, fisherman, but you can choose the way in which you'll die."

"Is that good news?" asked the fisherman. "Why do you wish to kill me? Is that your thanks for my having rescued you?"

"Choose how you'd like to die!" replied genie. "That is my thanks."

"But why?" the fisherman asked.

The Genie's Story

The genie answered the fisherman by saying, "Listen, and I'll tell you my story…

Long ago, I rebelled against King Solomon, the son of King David, so he sent one of his men to capture me. When I refused to obey him, he confined me in this brass jar, sealed it, and ordered it thrown deep into the sea. I prayed for someone to rescue me and pledged to make that person rich. But two hundred years went by, and I remained locked up in that dark, dank, cramped jar. I vowed to myself, "I will bestow the riches of the earth to the one who delivers me." But, another four hundred years passed, and still no one came to my rescue. Finally, I began to grow angry and said, "I'll kill the first person to open this jar." And then you came by and set me free.

"Just my luck! I would have to be the one who freed you!" the fisherman said.

"I'm sorry, but so it is," the genie replied. "Your death is your reward."

"Is this how you're going to repay me? A bad deed for a good one?" said the fisherman.

The Fisherman's Plan

The fisherman knew that he had to think fast, or he would soon be killed. He thought of his wife and children. He prayed to Allah, and then a possible way to outwit the genie occurred to him. "If only it would work," he thought.

"May I ask you one last question?" the fisherman said.

"Yes, but be quick about it," said the genie.

"By the Almighty's name, tell me if you were really inside this jar?" the fisherman asked.

"Of course, I was in there," the genie said.

"I think you're lying. That jar is not large enough for even one of your hands or feet. How could your whole body fit inside it?"

"I was inside. Don't you believe it?"

"No, I don't. Prove it to me."

Hearing this, the genie shook himself and turned back into a large wisp of smoke. Little by little, he coiled himself around like a snake and reentered the jar. When the smoke had disappeared, the genie shouted from within, "Fisherman, here I am in the jar. Do you believe me now?"

The fisherman at once took out the lead stopper and clamped it on the mouth of the jar. Then he cried out, "Genie, now tell me how you wish to die?"

"Spare me!" cried the genie. "Don't blame me for my actions. I was only joking with you. Be kind to me."

"You're lying! Why should I ever let you out? You insisted on killing me even though I set you free. I'm going to toss you back into the sea."

"Let me go free again and I swear that I'll never harm you. I'll make you rich."

"You're lying," said the fisherman.

But the fisherman eventually gave in to the genie's pleas for mercy. He made the genie pledge to be good to him if he let him out, and then he unfixed the lead stopper again. The smoke began to funnel into the sky and turned

Opposite: King Solomon was a wealthy and wise king in Israel between 970 and 931 BCE.

into a full-sized genie again. When he got completely out of the brass jar, the genie suddenly kicked it far out into the sea. The fisherman grew scared and trembled again, but the genie said: "Don't worry. Follow me, fisherman."

He took him to the far side of a mountain where they came to a tranquil lake in the middle of a vast wilderness. He ordered the fisherman to cast in his net. More fish swam here than the fisherman had ever seen. "Here you may fish peacefully," said the genie, "and you'll become rich, selling these rare delicacies to the king."

Scheherazade Finishes Telling the Tale of the Fisherman and the Genie

When morning came, Scheherazade lapsed into silence. The king wanted to hear more, but he needed to tend to the affairs of his kingdom, so he left, resolving to hear the rest of the story in the evening. Scheherazade's storytelling had kept the king distracted, and she had saved her own life.

Famous Stories Not from *The Arabian Nights*

The Arabian Nights is a collection of stories that Scheherazade is said to have told every night for one thousand nights to save herself and her people. Passed down orally for centuries before they were written down in the late 1200s, the stories originated in Persia. Throughout the ages, storytellers, editors, and translators have added to, deleted, and modified them. Today, they have come to include Arabian folktales, Indian fables, and Turkish anecdotes. The most authentic version of the tales surviving today is based on a 1300s Syrian manuscript housed in the Bibliothèque Nationale in Paris.

Many people think that the well-known and popular stories of "Sinbad the Sailor," "Aladdin and the Magic Lamp," and "Ali Baba and the Forty Thieves" come from *The Arabian Nights*, but it's not true. In fact, no one knows when or where these tales originated, but they became associated with *The Arabian Nights* when later translators and editors decided to include them among the tales. In truth, no definitive edition of *The Arabian Nights* exists today—and perhaps it never has.

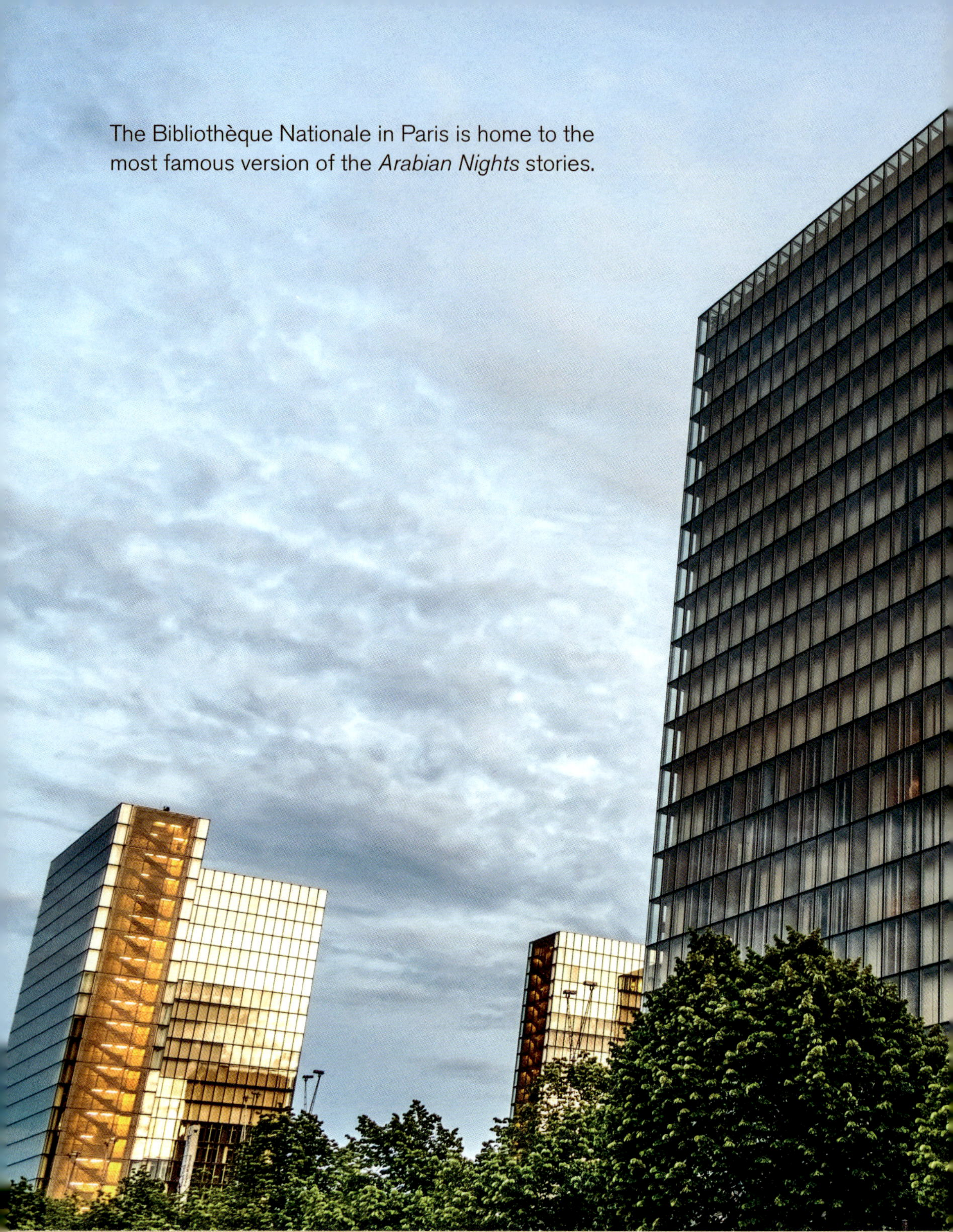

The Bibliothèque Nationale in Paris is home to the most famous version of the *Arabian Nights* stories.

QUAI
FRANÇOIS MAURIAC

5 The Traveler's Treasures

Many stories from around the world include a moral, or a lesson for readers to learn. Storytelling in the Middle East is no different. One story that includes a moral is called "The Traveler's Treasures."

Mohammed and Yubba in the Desert

Mohammed lived the best life a desert boy could live. Every day, Yubba, his father, went out to the pasture with the goats. Every day, Mohammed walked with him. When Yubba patted a goat on the head, Mohammed gently patted a different goat. When Yubba led the goats to the wadi (a stream that often runs only during the rainy season) to drink, Mohammed followed in his path, chasing straying goats back to the flock. When Yubba sat

Opposite: A goat herder at work in Turkey

back against a stone, Mohammed sat beside him. When Yubba told a story to while away the long afternoons, Mohammed listened and remembered.

Then, Yubba got sick. First, he did not go to the pasture, so Mohammed took the goats for him. Then he did not get out of bed, so Mohammed traded a goat for a warm blanket and food. Every evening, Mohammed brought his father soup and bread and sat by his bed. Often he told his father the stories that he remembered from the days they had shared in the pasture.

Finally, one day Yubba held Mohammed's hand and said, "My son, I am about to die. I have little to leave you. We have sold many of the goats. We have eaten most of our food, but listen carefully. My good advice I give you, and my advice is this: build for yourself houses in every part of the world."

Mohammed was a child, too small to build a house. He did not understand. How could he build houses in every part of the world? He had no money. He knew only how to herd goats, boil soup, and tell stories. "I will search for a wise man to explain my father's words," he thought. He gathered up his blanket, took one milk goat, and started out on the road at his front door.

Mohammed's Journey

Mohammed wandered for many years, making friends everywhere he went. First, he shared his goat's milk with a hungry little girl, who took him to her black tent, hidden behind the desert dunes. From her mother, he learned to make cheese, heating the milk until it curdled and then pressing the curds in a leather bag. The little girl's mother knew many things, but she did not know the answer to his father's good counsel—"Build houses in every part of the world."

Back Mohammed went to the road, gathering food from the fields and the woods. He cooked soup whenever he camped under the open sky, and he made cheese for his hosts whenever he stopped in a village. Once, he was attacked by robbers but cured their evil intent with kind words. He offered to share his food and his stories. In return, the robbers taught him how to read the secret paths in the woods and the desert. They even let him into their tree houses where they hid like monkeys in the deep forest. However, wise as they were in the wild ways, they did not know the answer to his father's advice—"Build houses in every part of the world."

Long, long years Mohammed wandered, sharing his gifts. He taught some people he met how to find the best pastures for their goats. He taught others how to make cheese and simmer soup. He taught still others how to read the secret paths of the creatures of the desert and woods. And everywhere, he told stories to make the children laugh and to touch the hearts of their parents.

Journey's End

One day, as he wandered, he felt the long wispy beard on his chin and heard his breath coming hard through his chest. He had become old and tired, and still he did not know the answer to his father's riddle. He followed the road until it became wider, filled with people and carts and camels. Finally, he came to the largest city he had ever seen, topped by the **minarets** of the **mosque**. Humbly, he made his way to the mosque in the center of the city. He approached the wise **imam**, whose beard was shorter than Mohammed's own, and told his story. Then he asked once again, "What did my father mean? How am I to build houses in every part of the world?"

The old imam gazed long at Mohammed's face, now lined with wrinkles, and reached out his hand to the tired old man. "You have done exactly what your father asked," said the imam. "Have you not made friends everywhere? Is not your friend's house your own? You are welcome wherever you go. Every house you visit is your own."

Moral: There is nothing so noble as to travel and make friends.

This mosque in Yemen has the typical architectural style of mosques, including domes and tall minarets.

Futteh Ali Shah.

W.

by Sir Robert Ker Porter.

6 Other Middle Eastern Legends

Kai Kaus, shah of ancient Persia, was not noted for being a great king. In fact, he was said to have been rather foolish. But he will long be remembered for his legendary flight. From his youth Kai Kaus had been fascinated by the heavens. One fine spring day, he sent for his astronomers to tell them of his plan.

The King Who Wanted to Fly

"I have thought of a way to fly," Kai Kaus said, "to see for myself the nature of the sun and moon and how it is that night follows day. I will study the planets and the stars that surround them. Nothing like this has ever been planned until now!" The shah's eyes shone with excitement.

His astronomers stared at him in astonishment. Kai Kaus laughed to see their expressions. Then he said, "I have had four young eagles stolen from their nest and

Opposite: This illustration shows Fatteh Ali Shah, King of Persia. He was second king of Iran, ruling from 1797 to 1834.

raised to be large and strong. My carpenter has built a framework of aloe wood. I will sit in it, and the eagles will carry me to heights no one has seen before."

The first astronomer spoke. "Your Majesty, even if this would work, you will go neither high nor far."

"We can't know that, can we?" said Kai Kaus angrily.

"You'll be dragged," said the second astronomer. "Have someone else try this flight first."

"No," replied Kai Kaus. "I want to be the first to fly!"

The third astronomer stroked his beard. "People were not meant to fly," he said.

"Silence," ordered the shah. "I have heard enough."

A few days later one of Queen Sudaveh's handmaidens looked out the window of the women's quarters. "My queen," she said, "the shah is preparing to take flight."

Sudaveh looked out. What she saw caused her to lift her skirts and run down the stairs to the courtyard. She pushed her way through a gathering crowd.

Kai Kaus's Flying Throne

Kai Kaus had ordered a special chair fitted into the aloe-wood frame. Attached to it were high poles with little harnesses tied to the ends. Beside the chair lay an extra-long javelin with a chunk of raw meat tied to the end. In cages on the ground crouched the four eagles.

"My dear," said the queen anxiously, "what are you doing?"

"Rejoice," replied Kai Kaus. "Today, my dream comes true. Today, I fly like an eagle." He jumped into the chair and settled himself.

"You'll be killed!" exclaimed Queen Sudaveh. "Stop him, someone!"

But no one dared.

At the shah's command, servants wearing leather gloves took the eagles from their cages and climbed up to fasten them into the leather harnesses attached to the poles. The eagles thrashed about and screeched, beating their wings wildly.

"Stand back," ordered the shah. "Now hand me that pole with the meat."

A servant jumped to obey. Kai Kaus dangled the meat in front of one eagle and then another until all strained to reach it. He lifted the pole. The framework scraped on the ground and then jerkily began to rise. Watchers gasped as the strange contraption narrowly missed the palace wall.

Taking Flight

Over the palm trees flew the eagles, intent on the meat. On the wind came the sound of laughter. Clearly, the shah was enjoying his flight. Shading their eyes against the sun, the people watched as the fliers got smaller and smaller until they faded from view.

"Foolish man," said Sudaveh. "What will he do when he comes down? Guards! Call our fastest horsemen to pursue him. Call Rustem, the king's champion, to lead them. Make haste!"

Shah Kai Kaus was still laughing. The eagles had given up trying to reach the meat and seemed to be flying for the pure joy of it.

"At last," said the shah, "at last I am flying. What a sensation! Even more wonderful than I imagined."

Down below, people looked as small as insects, and a village, the size of a child's toy. Kai Kaus glanced up at the sun, but the light hurt his eyes. The bright orb seemed as far away as ever.

The eagles flew east, glad to be free and never tiring. Now Kai Kaus looked down on mountaintops, seeing, as if in miniature, the paths of camel drivers and lakes like tiny mirrors in the sun.

The scene beneath Kai Kaus may have looked like this until he got too high up!

Disappointment and Danger

It was cold now, and Kai Kaus wished he had worn heavier robes. He dropped the meat, which plummeted to the ground far below, but the eagles flew on. After dark, it grew even colder. The shah strained to see the stars. He was disappointed to observe that they looked the same as they had from the palace. When the moon came up, it too looked the same, no closer than ever. Kai Kaus shook from disappointment as well as the bitter cold. Surely the eagles would land soon.

Hour after hour, they flew on. Suddenly the frame jerked, and Kai Kaus grabbed tightly to keep from falling. The eagles had tired and were thrashing and spiraling toward the earth.

The frame landed with a bump, broke apart, and sent the shah sprawling. Fortunately, he had landed in desert sand and, while scraped and bruised, he was not seriously injured.

He caught hold of the frame and wrapped his arms in his robes to protect himself from the eagles' beaks and talons.

This illustration from an old Persian manuscript shows Kai Kaus being carried by eagles.

With a knife he had strapped to his leg, he cut the birds loose. They flapped away into the darkness.

Kai Kaus now saw himself to be in great danger. He had no idea where he was or how he was to get home. No one, he realized, knew where to search for him. He drew his garments about his bruised body and curled up on the sand to await the dawn.

A Band of Thieves

With the first orange rays of the sun, Kai Kaus found himself alone in a vast desert. There was nothing to eat, and what was worse, nothing to drink. He knew he must put the morning sun to his back and walk to the west toward home.

For two days he trudged, suffering from the heat of the day and the chill of the night. On the third day, dazed and ill, he came upon a band of desert thieves. The shah could not understand their language, nor they his. However, they judged by his fine clothes that Kai Kaus was a rich man and that they might collect ransom for him. They gave him water and food and let him rest in one of their tents. Some of them set out across the desert for the nearest city.

Meanwhile, when the king's champion, Rustem, was summoned, he shook his head in disbelief at the shah's latest folly. Then he readied himself and his great yellow horse for travel. Taking the best horsemen on the fastest horses, he rode to the east.

And so one morning Kai Kaus looked up from the campfire and rubbed his eyes in astonishment. There on a sand dune stood a great yellow horse, rearing on his hind legs and pawing the air, his mane flying in the wind, and on his back sat the broad-chested Rustem. Before the startled thieves could do more than grab their swords, the horsemen were in the camp. All the thieves might have been slain if Kai Kaus had not cried out, "Let them go! If they had not helped me, my bones would be bleaching in the sun."

The thieves ran off into the desert, and Kai Kaus welcomed his valiant men.

No Regrets?

By the time the party got back to the palace, Shah Kai Kaus had almost recovered from his ordeal. He ordered a grand banquet and a celebration to last three days in honor of Rustem and his men.

When at last Kai Kaus was alone with Queen Sudaveh, she said, "I suppose you will be raising eagles for your next flight."

"Do you think I'm crazy?" he answered. "I could have been killed. Someone should have stopped me."

"Of course," said Sudaveh indulgently, patting his arm. "People were not meant to fly."

"Oh yes, they were, my dear," said Kai Kaus, "and let it be written that I was the first to fly!"

Hodja and the Hungry Coat: A Turkish Tale

Hen Hodja arrived home late one fall afternoon, with dirt all over his patched trousers, his faded shirt, and his tattered felt cap. He'd been laboring in the vineyards since sunrise.

"Hurry! Change your clothes and bathe," said his wife, Fatima. "You'll be late for the grand banquet at the **emir**'s!"

"I can't be late," declared Hodja, washing his hands and splashing water on his face. "I'll have to go in these clothes."

Pages 54–55: An illustration from the 1500s shows what a typical banquet thrown by an emir might have looked like.

Fatima frowned and brushed dirt from his trousers. Then Hodja climbed on Zeki, his little donkey, and waved goodbye.

Hodja Makes His Entrance

As he approached the emir's mansion, Hodja admired the candles gleaming in the many windows. Music and bits of conversations drifted through the crisp air, and heavy footsteps and laughter echoed in the courtyard as the men arrived for the banquet. Hodja tethered Zeki and joined the well-dressed crowd inside.

Servants circled the reception room carrying trays of sweetmeats and cups of tea. Hodja greeted other guests, but not one spoke to him in return. People turned their backs or swept past, barely glancing his way.

Soon the emir announced that the banquet was ready. Groups of chattering guests pressed through the doorway and sat at low tables where soup was waiting for them. Hodja, not wanting to be jostled in the crowd, stood waiting in a dark corner of the candlelit room.

The emir glanced briefly in Hodja's direction and clapped his hands to call a servant. "Who admitted that dirty laborer in patched trousers?" the emir whispered to the man. "Get rid of him."

The dark-eyed servant grabbed Hodja's arm and pulled him outside.

"I'm going, I'm going," said Hodja, "but you may see me again."

He climbed on Zeki and plodded home.

Hodja Has a Plan

"What happened?" asked Fatima. When he told her, she cried, "Oh, my poor dear!"

"Don't worry," Hodja said. "I have a plan. Bring me basins of hot water and soap, my new shoes, and my best shirt, trousers, turban, and coat."

He soaped and scrubbed himself, then donned his festive clothes, a perfectly wound turban, and his fine coat.

Fatima kissed him. "Is that still you, Hodja?"

"Yes, indeed," he replied. "And now I will return to the banquet."

As before, he tethered Zeki in the courtyard and walked toward the house. In the doorway stood the dark-eyed servant who had thrown Hodja out.

The servant bowed. "Welcome. It is a pleasure to see you, **effendi**. Allow me to escort you."

Hodja smiled and followed the servant into the banquet room. Heads turned as he was led toward the emir. Guests whispered.

"Come, Hodja Effendi," called the emir, "sit here beside me in the place of honor. The soup is finished, but there will be other courses for your pleasure."

"Thank you," Hodja replied as he sat on a cushion at the low table.

Soon trays of lamb shish kebab, rice pilaf, vegetables, cheeses, and breads were passed. Hodja filled his plate. Then he picked up several pieces of lamb and a handful of rice and tucked the food into his left coat pocket.

"Eat, coat, eat!" commanded Hodja.

He picked up a fistful of vegetables, a slice of bread, and a wedge of cheese. He stuffed them into his right coat pocket.

"Eat, coat, eat!" commanded Hodja.

All the guests stared at him.

"Tell me, Hodja Effendi," said the emir, "why are you feeding your coat?"

"When I came to your banquet wearing my work clothes, you threw me out," declared Hodja. "Now I'm wearing my fine coat, and you welcome me. It must be the coat, then, that you invited to your banquet, not me."

The emir's face flushed with shame. Other guests lowered their eyes and stared at their laps.

"Ah, here comes dessert!" cried Hodja. "Before I leave, my coat would love to savor pieces of sweet baklava and perhaps a cup of rich coffee."

Baklava is made from dough, chopped nuts, and honey.

Glossary

Allah The name for God in the religion of Islam.

Babylon A large city in ancient Mesopotamia.

caliph An old name for the chief Muslim civil and religious ruler.

civilization A society that has an advanced level of social development and organization.

constellation A group of stars that form a pattern and are named for their form and for mythological beings.

continent Any of Earth's seven very large landmasses. The continents are Antarctica, Africa, Asia, Europe, North America, South America, and Australia.

effendi In Mediterranean or Arab countries, a person who is highly educated or has a high social standing.

emir The Muslim title for a ruler or military commander.

imam A prayer leader at a mosque.

Mesopotamia An ancient civilization centered around the Tigris and Euphrates rivers.

minarets The tower of a mosque.

mosque A Muslim place of worship.

Muslim A person who follows the religion of Islam. Muslims believe in one god called Allah.

myths Legends or stories that typically concern the origins of a people or explain natural or societal phenomenon and will often include gods or supernatural beings.

pantheon The name for all the gods of a people or country as a collection.

Persia An empire that became modern-day Iran.

shah The king. The term was formerly used in Iran.

Sumer A Mesopotamian civilization.

vizier In ancient Egypt, this was the highest ranking official next to the ruler.

Further Information

Books

Schomp, Virginia. *The Ancient Persians*. New York: Cavendish Square Publishing, 2009.

Storm, Rachel. *Mythology of Egypt and the Middle East: Myths and Legends of Egypt, Persia, Asia Minor, Sumer, and Babylon*. Leicestershire, UK: Anness Publishing, 2003.

Walker, Barbara K. *A Treasury of Turkish Folktales for Children*. Hamden, CT: Linnet Books, 1998.

Websites

Ancient Civilizations: Mesopotamia

http://www.mesopotamia.co.uk/staff/resources/background/bg20/home.html

Learn more about Mesopotamian culture and mythology on this site hosted by the British Museum.

Geography: An Ancient and Modern Crossroads

http://www.pbs.org/wgbh/globalconnections/mideast/themes/geography

PBS presents a fantastic summary of the geography of the Middle East, including pictures and links.

Scheherazade Interactives

http://creativekidseducationfoundation.org/kids/sche/base.htm

Find information about Persian art, Middle Eastern geography, and storytelling on this interactive website, which includes music from the composer Rimsky-Korsakov's symphony *Scheherazade*.

Index

Page numbers in **boldface** are illustrations.
Entries in **boldface** are glossary terms.